G000255515

Bygone
CROWBOROUGH

Bygone
CROWBOROUGH

Malcolm Payne
and
Luther Batchelor

Phillimore

1987

Published by
PHILLIMORE & CO. LTD.
Shopwyke Hall, Chichester, Sussex

ISBN 0 85033 647 3

Printed and bound in Great Britain by
BIDDLES LTD.
Guildford, Surrey

List of Illustrations

All photographs are from the Luther Batchelor collection, with the exception of that of the authors on the jacket which is by John Sharp.

Historical Introduction

Crowborough is a sprawling country town on the eastern edge of Ashdown Forest. It developed from a number of hamlets which expanded to become villages and, at the turn of the century, began to knit together into the town we know today. Most buildings in the town centre are relatively modern, many being Victorian or early Edwardian, but a few are at least 250 years old.

It must be assumed that the earliest human inhabitants of the area hunted on the heath, though little evidence of their activity has been found except for a few flint arrowheads on the western slopes of Crowborough Common. Many more remains have been found in the surrounding Ashdown Forest, such as flint arrow and axe heads, scrapers, and monoliths, as reported in 1974 by C. F. Tebbutt F.S.A. in *Sussex Archaeological Collections, 112*. The Wealden Iron Research Group has discovered evidence of Roman and Saxon iron working in the vicinity – many small bloomeries have been excavated in wood and heathland all around Crowborough and archaeologists feel many more will come to light in the future. These bloomeries reveal themselves by their heaps of cinder slag which over the years may have become covered in vegetation.

The earliest written documentation of the village seems to be in the Domesday survey [insert Latin line from Phillimore edition] which mentions Alchornes Manor in Crowborough: 'William of Keynes holds 1 virgate of this manor. It is at Alchin.' No value is given for the land. A virgate is a measurement of land, usually one-quarter of a hide. In Sussex hides were variable, since the area was linked with value; 30 acres of good farming land could constitute one hide, as could up to 200 acres of waste or heathland. This Domesday entry classifies the manor as land belonging to the Archbishop of Canterbury in the Hundred of South Malling. The land was in fact in the parish of Buxted and therefore in both the Hundred and Deanery of South Malling.

The next piece of written evidence relates to Crowborough's oldest house, Luxford Farm, which is still inhabited today. This must have been the manor house and a mention in an Assize Roll (housed in the Public Record Office) shows that in 1279 it was the home of Bartholomew de Luggesford. The original building is a perfect example of a Sussex longhouse, though the thatched roof has long since been replaced by tiles, and floors and ceilings have been built which hide the high roof. Blackened timbers can still be seen in the bedrooms, proof of the smoke which once made its way through the roof from the hearth at one end of the large hall. It seems probable that the hall was divided into two rooms and then a cross division created a third room, as is usual in 13th-century longhouses. In later years a big open fireplace was added, with a wide chimney, allowing upstairs rooms to be created. Structural additions were made from the 14th century right up to the 19th century, when the Goldsmiths Company gave the building a completely new facade, so that it now looks like a typical Victorian farmhouse.

In 1292 we find a reference to Crowborough's first religious establishment. This was a chapel in ruins on 'the waste of Cranbergh' which the Archbishop of Canterbury, Pecham (or Peckham), records as having been at 'Gelderegge', today's

Gilridge or Gillridge. Peckham gave two acres of land at 'Scherche juxta Gelderegge' for a new chapel and cemetery in recompense for the one-acre site of the ruined chapel. It is not known whether this new chapel was ever built, though there is a Church Field near Gilridge today and some mounds near it, referred to as 'The Cemetery' by locals. A document known as the 'Inquisitions of the Nonce', dated 1342, by which time one could reasonably expect the new chapel to have been completed, notes John de Gilderigge as a parishioner of Withyham, a nearby church which residents of Crowborough attended as their own chapel was ruined. It may be, therefore, that Gilridge chapel was never erected. Gilridge, Church Field and Luxford Farm are all within an area of about half a square mile and the fact that they are all mentioned in 13th-century documents suggests that they may have been part of an integrated community from that time if not earlier.

The inhabitants of Crowborough's hamlets probably attended churches in various different parishes, depending on their location. Those to the north and north-east would have attended Withyham, those in the west and south-west, including Alchornes Manor, would have attended Buxted, and those in the south and south-east, Rotherfield.

The spelling of Crowborough has varied considerably over the centuries. The 1390 Minister's Accounts refer to the community as 'Crowbergh' and Duchy of Lancaster documents of 1564 record the spelling variously as 'Croweborowghe Gate' and 'Crowbarow'. This is not surprising as spelling was by no means fixed at that time, being purely phonetic. In 1570 Lambarde published a history of Kent, illustrated by a map showing beacons in the county and in parts of Sussex. One of the outlying beacons marked is at 'Crowbarow'. Originally, warning beacons were simply large bonfires built on the ground but, later, iron baskets or cressettes were fixed on to poles and pitch was added to the vegetation to help ignition and give a long-lasting blaze. Crowborough Beacon dates from this time, and is ideally situated as the highest land in the area, 796 feet above sea level.

The most detailed picture of Crowborough in Elizabethan times is drawn for us by the 'Buckhurst Terrier' of 1597. This was an inventory of the 17 manors belonging to the Barony of Buckhurst, including Alchornes Manor: 'The p'ticuler Survey of all land and singuler ye Lands, Tenements, and other Hereditaments to ye saide Manor of Alchornes.' The Baron of Buckhurst at this time was Thomas Sackville, whose ancestor, Herbrand de Sackville, came to England from Normandy with William the Conqueror. The word terrier, meaning an inventory or register of a landed estate, derives from the Latin word for land, *terra*. A study of this survey reveals many farm, house, field and owners' names which still exist in the area today. The survey was built into the library wall at Buckhurst and did not come to light again until 1931, which accounts for the fact that it has not been used as source material by earlier local historians. The original document can now be seen in the East Sussex Record Office at Lewes.

There are many possible explanations for the etymology of the name Crowborough. The first known written version of the name appears in Archbishop Peckham's register of 1292 as 'Cranbergh'. 'Cran' probably means large (as in the French *grand*, or the Gaelic *crann* meaning a measure, usually of herrings), and 'bergh' means hill, so the name could mean 'big hill'. Later spellings are all variants of 'Crowbarrow', thought to mean 'hill of crows'. Other possible origins are 'croh' which describes the colour saffron and may be a reference to the local clay or gorse bloom, so that Crowborough would mean 'a saffron-coloured hill'. The only constant is the interpretation of 'barrow', 'bergh' and 'borough' as hill. A final theory relates to the gift of '3,000 hides by Ashdown' in A.D. 648, mentioned in the Anglo-Saxon Chronicle, by King Cenwald of Wessex to his kinsman, Cuthred. The land, including the high land in the area, might have been named after the giver, making it 'Cenwahl's Bergh', which might have been abbreviated by 1292 to 'Cranbergh'.

By the 16th and 17th centuries there were at least two ironworking centres in the area, one near Mardens Hill and the other near Maynards Gate. The latter site was excavated by the Sussex Archaeological Society in 1975-76 and the report can be seen in *Sussex Archaeological Collections, 116*. At Mardens Hill, on a site between Jinks Hole, Virgil's Bridge and New Mill, the retaining banks of the massive bay pond are still visible. The feed stream still runs through but the pond has long since dried up. The water would once have turned a wheel which in turn worked the bellows of the blast furnace. Lower down can be seen the banks of the hammer pond which turned a wheel to power the huge hammer of the forge.

There would have been other industries active at the same time: charcoal burning to support the iron furnaces, farming, milling, and probably pottery as there is much clay locally. There is no written evidence of the latter craft, but mills and farms are mentioned in the Buckhurst Terrier. Spinning and weaving would have been carried on as small cottage industries and most communities would have been self-supporting.

A local notable, Sir Henry Fermor, died in 1734 and in his will endowed a charity to instigate the building of a chapel and a school. All Saints' church, on Chapel Hill, was completed in 1744 and the original school building is now the vicarage. Sir Henry's generosity is still commemorated, however, by the Sir Henry Fermor school, now a little distance from the original site, on Crowborough Hill.

A tithe schedule and map of the area was drawn up in 1842 and copies can be viewed at the East Sussex Record Office in Lewes. By the mid-19th century the Crowborough area consisted of small fields and woodlands, interspersed with small villages and hamlets. Crowborough Cross appears as Willets Cross and is treated as a separate area. All around Crowborough Hill are names of great interest to the local historian, such as Poundfield, Steel Cross, Cooks (or Crooks) Corner, Crowborough Town, Beacon Hill, Alchornes, Coldharbour, Walshes, Jarvis Brook and Chapel Green. All appear to be of ancient origin and each area seems to have been considered as a separate and independent community.

The opening of the railway in 1868 stimulated the growth of agriculture and horticulture as fresh produce could be transported to the London markets. In 1890 Dr. Leeson Prince wrote a book on Crowborough, praising its fresh air, views and good food. He distributed his book free of charge to colleagues throughout the country and soon Crowborough was inundated both by invalids and those merely interested to see the town. Houses and hotels had to be built rapidly and many service industries developed to cope with the visitors arriving by every train. Many stayed on, had houses built and became permanent residents.

Other visitors came to Crowborough, particularly from London, for shooting weekends. The Goldsmiths Company bought up many local estates, some on the Marquis of Abergavenny's land and some on Lord de la Warr's property. Farms, woods and meadows were all improved to make good working estates which would also provide excellent shooting land. Select housing estates were built on some of the land, served by the new railway line which brought Crowborough so much nearer to London. Horticulture and dairy farming expanded and new employment prospects were opened up for gardeners and domestic staff. More and more photographs were taken at this time as the plate camera was developing, and from these we can see the Crowborough High Street and Cross area gradually taking on a more urbanised aspect. The name Henry Ambrose Stickells is synonymous with the early development of photography in Crowborough.

Stickells was born in Cranbrook in Kent. When he reached his teens he was given a little money, some photographic equipment and a horse-drawn trailer-cum-caravan by his father. The van had living accommodation as well as a darkroom and studio. He worked his way, perhaps unconsciously, towards Crowborough, marrying en route, his eldest daughter being born in Leigh. Eventually he arrived in Crowborough and was welcomed by the residents, as many as could afford it having their photograph taken by him. He did very well for himself, working initially from his van, and was soon able to move into premises in Croft Road which are now occupied by Chappell's chemist shop. He soon had a house specially built for him in the same road, fronted by a shop and with a studio and darkroom at the rear. The site is now occupied by Bysouth's Funeral Directors and a gift shop, but the initials 'AHS' and the date 1902 can still be seen high on one of the walls. Over the years Stickells produced some of Crowborough's best picture postcards, now highly sought after by collectors. He also photographed almost every person and event of note in the town and has left an invaluable record of the development of streets, shops and houses, many of which have now disappeared.

Through Stickells's camera lens we have a privileged view into the past and can see the original Crowborough Beacon golf clubhouse, built in 1895 and demolished in 1907, and the majestic *Beacon Hotel*, now replaced by bungalows in Mill Lane and Beacon Road. The luxury evident in shots of the interior of the *Beacon* helps us to understand why so many visitors were attracted to stay there or in one of the other hotels which abounded in the Beacon area.

Stickells also captured many charming school scenes. Some residential schools developed in Crowborough, wealthy parents being persuaded that their children would thrive in the good air of the town. The earliest educational establishment was probably the charity school, followed by St John's school, which opened in 1840, two years after St John's church. There were nonconformist chapels as well as parish churches. The Baptists claim to have had a chapel in the town as early as 1650, and the Wesleyans, Plymouth Brethren and Salvation Army all built churches around the hill. There was a Congregational chapel, known as Starvell's, in Tubwell Lane, Jarvis Brook. Meetings were first held in a barn, but a purpose-built chapel was erected later. However, as early as 1910 this fell into disrepair and now only a few graves in the grass mark the site. Jarvis Brook School was also held in a barn in Western Road in its early days, on a site now occupied by Hastingford Villa. Later, in 1885, a school was built at the western end of this road which doubled as a church until St Michael's was finished in 1906. Forest Fold Baptist chapel also began life as a barn, though this was gradually converted into a more suitable building. National schools were opened at Steel Cross, Poundgate and Whitehill. Many of Stickells's photographs show the pupils in their Victorian dress standing rigidly still for the required time while the lens was open. It is hard to pick out the original buildings today as so many additions and alterations have been made. Beacon School, on the Beeches Estate and in Green Lane, is now one of the largest comprehensive school in Europe.

Crowborough has grown rapidly since the Second World War, especially after its potential as a commuter area was recognised in 1950. When all the latest housing estates are finished and occupied, it is estimated that the town's population will be 24,000, just over three times what it was in 1950. People now have much more time for leisure activities than they had in the past. In Victorian times working men's clubs and church clubs supplied all that men required after a long working week, but today our requirements are much more sophisticated. Crowborough has responded with the Goldsmiths Leisure Centre, completed in 1985, which has football and hockey pitches, an athletics track and a large caravan park. This has developed on a site given for recreation purposes by the Goldsmiths Company in 1936. The Wolfe ground in Blackness, given by Miss Wolfe, a descendant of the famous General Wolfe of Quebec, still thrives and provides some facilities not found at Goldsmiths. Much leisure-time activity is now channelled into charity work and there are many local groups actively at work in various fields.

The authors hope that the following pictures will put flesh on the bones of this short account of the town, bring it to life and give hours of entertainment and pleasure to every reader.

Stickells

1.   Ambrose Henry Stickells, one of Crowborough's most outstanding photographers of Victorian times. Most of the illustrations in this book are his work. His father had been one of the pioneers of early photography, cutting glass for plates which he then coated. At this time development was by sunlight, and even Ambrose Henry put his contact prints out on a long ladder in daylight.

2. The horse-drawn van given to Stickells by his father, in which he travelled from Cranbrook, eventually arriving in Crowborough to move into his first house in this town, a cottage in New Road, now demolished.

3. Stickells's shop in Croft Road, the frieze advertising a competition for Kodak snaps with a £1,000 prize. In the left-hand window a box camera is offered at 12s. 6d. and safety roll film is shown for the public's use. By this time, c.1920, photography was becoming a hobby for the masses.

Street Scenes

4. Typical of Stickells's work of the 1800s is this picture of Crowborough High Street looking north. In the foreground a road can be seen entering from the right; this was Tubwell Lane, now New Road, and the large kitchen garden next to it is now the site of Woolworth's.

5. Crowborough High Street in 1901. Looking south, Rush the butcher's, which is still there, can be seen in the distance. A horse and cart heads into the distant Broadway and a delivery boy rests with his heavy bicycle before making the steep pull up Beacon Road.

6. This early picture of Crowborough Cross (*c.*1872) shows Turk's shop on the site of today's Barclays Bank; at this time the inn on the right had no bay windows or east wing.

7. Looking north from the High Street in 1897. Booker and Filtness's shop has evolved from Turk's store. A wonderful array of trugs hangs from the blind-bar, and the Victorian delivery hand-cart stands outside the shop. A potential customer seems to be checking if he can afford something he has seen on display.

8. The Cross, *c.*1890, looking rather like a frontier town in the colonies. Rice Bros. saddlers on the left was managed by Arthur Bradley, with his brother Tom in the tailor's shop above. Between them, as a good advertisement, they dressed the minute Jackie Lambert, shown in photograph 109.

9. How deserted Crowborough Cross and High Street look in this photograph, so different from the traffic-light controlled bustle seen today. The hitching-post indicates the leisurely pace of traffic at the main cross-roads, when it was still known as Willetts Cross.

10. Looking north from Crowborough Hill towards the Broadway. Driving the horse-drawn van is a baker, and the old man with the beard and Gladstone bag is thought to be Ebenezer Littleton, the Baptist Minister – his chapel is in the left foreground. Prams appear to be very tall or close to the ground, and gas lamps were few and far between in 1910.

11. Crowborough Broadway *c.*1917. Most of the men would have been away at the front, and the village has a very deserted appearance. In the distance to the right is Boro' Cycle Works where bicycles were actually manufactured.

12.   Croft Road and an estate agent's office reveals that the town is beginning to grow. To the right is Ravenscroft, but only the large gates of this big boarding-house can be seen. It was one of dozens that sprang up to cater for the many visitors who arrived after Dr. Leeson Prince recommended Crowborough as a health resort in his book in 1890.

13.   Croft Road in 1925, showing a postman making deliveries from his cart. In the right foreground we can just make-out a sign advertising 'Pratt's Motor Spirit', whilst the large pocket watch shows just where the watchmaker had premises.

14. Crowborough Hill, then Station Road, with Crowborough in the distance dominated by Pratt's Mill. The fields in front of it were known as Pratt's Bottom.

15. Even in 1925 Beacon Road has only one motor-car parked beside the public house and two people are able to stand in the middle of the main road talking. On the right was the field which eight years later was to be the site of the big main post office. All the trees give the village centre the appearance of a country lane.

Employment

16. Mr. Pentecost the Crowborough postman in the early 1900s. He blew his horn for people to come out and collect letters.

17. Crowborough Cross in the early 1900s. Squeezed between the butcher's shop and the provision and hardware shop is the village's first post office – Mr. Pentecost would have worked from here. To the right is Turk's drapery, and in the distant background Aubin's hardware, smithy, and farriers.

18.   Greenyer's Stores in London Road, *c.* 1908. This was Crowborough's second post office. There is now a travel booking office and the Haywards Heath Building Society on the site.

19.   Staff stand proudly in front of Booker's General Stores in Jarvis Brook, and the small but neat post office echoes the design of the one in Crowborough Cross, shown in plate 17.

20. Beacon Road post office being built in 1925. The speed notice shows only 10 m.p.h., and the blur of the charabanc shows just how slow were film coatings and shutter speeds in those days.

21. Crowborough G.P.O. staff posing outside their new post office in Beacon Road, *c.* 1926.

22. Chapel Green Stores, *c*. 1910, showing Mr. Vigor with his staff and horse-drawn van. Crowborough's first bank was housed in this building, customers being served through an outside window.

23. Other than London when it became accessible by rail, local shops were the only outlet for local produce. The Clock House Dairy in the High Street retailed local eggs, butter and milk. The Fernbank Complex is now on the site, with the old Clock House clock-casing on top of one of the buildings.

24. As people had to stand rigidly still because of the slow speed of camera plates, photographing premises became quite an occasion. Here we can see how long it must have taken to set up three milk floats and a push-cart in front of Palmer's Dairy in the High Street. This is now Guest's shoe shop.

25. Whitehill, showing Tingley's clothier's store built of corrugated iron. Most of the other buildings are of local stone. A farmer's cart goes down the hill in the distance, probably to Coldharbour Farm.

26. Dier's shop in the High Street was the main off-licence. It would have supplied wines and spirits to the gentry and ale to the cottagers. This shop was still Dier's until 1985, when the death of Clive Dier made it necessary for the business to close.

27. Frank Charlton was a seedsman, but also a fruiterer and greengrocer. Shops in Sussex for miles around were proud to label greengrocery as 'Crowborough grown'.

28. As can be seen, many local shops had frontage and facilities equal to any town shop, and local businessmen were quick to advertise their goods in every possible way. This horse was probably about to pull its decorated cart from W. T. Baker's shop in Whitehill to join one of Crowborough's carnival parades.

29. Featherstone and Jacques' bakery van. The shop was in Crowborough High Street.

30. Samuel Taylor and his son George Taylor dealt in building materials, coal and coke, and acted as hauliers. This shows the firm's lorry in 1926. The business continues today, still in the hands of the Taylor family.

31. The Model T Ford van of W. Wilmshurst and Sons, who ran the mills in Jarvis Brook for 99 years, from 1885 to 1984. The vehicle stands in front of Paige's coachworks, Croham Road, now the site of Studlands Caravans. Most of the beautiful hand-painted lettering and scroll-work seen on old vans was done at this works.

32. Jim and Charley Aubin at Aubin's smithy in London Road in the early 1900s. Since that time there has been a pottery, a craft shop and wedding outfitters on the site.

33. Some of the horses that would have been shod at Aubin's. These are Connor Brothers' horses hauling a timber-tug in Crowborough Warren in 1920, with Albert Taylor and Fred Croft in charge. The house in the background is Warren Wood.

34. Nimmy Adams at the age of 17, hatching (cleaning off moss and other dross) flawed bark ready for use in the tannery. Dried bark was broken into small pieces, which were then sewn into hessian sacks with a large piece of bark stitched into the sack-mouth. When empty sacks were returned from the tannery at Edenbridge, they usually contained some leather with which the men soled their boots.

35.   Jack Tasker and Luther Maynard in woods near New Mill, filling sacks with fresh charcoal. The fork-like tool being used is known as a charcoal spud, and also serves as a sieve or riddle.

36.   Jack Tasker and his son Jack, charcoal burning. The wood had to be neatly and precisely stacked and then burnt very slowly. The barrows were all home-made.

37. Mr. Frost cleaving hazel wands in preparation for making hoops. Barrels made of rough wooden slats would be held together by these hoops, and held almost every commodity we now get in cardboard cases, from apples to hats. Coopers's barrels had iron hoops, and they were made water-tight.

38. Jack Hoath of Friar's Gate carries armsful of hoops to stack. Each man appears to do his chosen job and, by the look of the tall stacks, their work must have been in great demand. The shed roofs were thatched with left-over shavings from the hazel wands.

39. Dick Price (centre) using a stone axe to dress stone in Hurtis Hill quarry Dressed stone in the foreground is stacked as a dry run for a chimney, each stone having its special place.

40. Building workers posed in front of their wooden scaffold. They are thought to be Connor Brothers' men working on Mayfield College, a building with quite a lot of special stone-work.

41. This part of Crowborough High Street shows a large quantity of local stone in the buildings, but many of the Victorian buildings were of locally-made brick. There were at least six brick-yards in the area in these times, two in the Park Road area, one at Cooks Corner, one in St John's, one in Alderbrook, and the largest in Jarvis Brook.

42. Crowborough Brick Yard in Jarvis Brook, the longest surviving, and the largest, being in production for around 100 years. Here we see brickmakers, claydiggers, burners, and loaders as they were in the late 19th century.

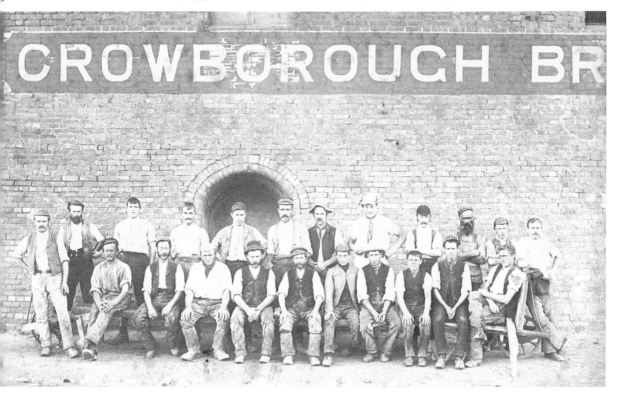

43. Pratt's Mill, just south of Croham Road, built by Richard Pratt in 1861. He brought the mill by horse-drawn timbertug from Tunbridge Wells. In 1862 his son Jesse was killed by catching his round-frock in the machinery while dressing millstones. The mill house (right) was built some time before the mill and is now known as Mill Cottage. The mill itself has since been converted into a house.

44. Beacon Mill in Mill Lane, which was built in 1782 and burnt down in 1943. Originally painted white, it was later tarred black and embellished with an open Victorian belvedere (pavilion) from which the view could be admired. Teas were also sold in the lower round-house. Throughout most of the Victorian period it was worked by members of the Pratt family.

45. New Mill, Crowborough Warren, built by Edward Frisby Howis. It was here in 1840 that the flour for Queen Victoria's wedding cake was ground, the wheat having been grown at Redgate Mill, on the south-eastern side of the hill. The cottage to the right, now demolished, was the birthplace of Nimmy Adams (see plate 34).

6. New Mill Pond's centre sluice. The mill itself is just out of view but we can see Miss Daisy Stickells and her two brothers, Ambrose and Percy, both of whom were later to become photographers, Ambrose having premises in Tunbridge Wells, and Percy in St Leonards.

Farming

47. Charlie Price of Coldharbour Farm. The young boy being introduced to the calf is thought to be Tom Price his grandson. Earlier an old inn, known as the *Naked Lady*, had stood on the site of this farm; now it is occupied by Herne School.

48.   Men going hop-picking to Horsmonden, where they would stay for the duration of the pick, two to three weeks. Hops were also picked by local folk who walked to nearby gardens each day. This picture is taken outside the stable yard in Crowborough Cross.

49.   Mrs. Stickells with her two daughters, Daisy and Irene, and a daughter of a tenant farmer, Walters, hop-picking at Hoadley's Farm in the St John's area. Parts of this farm are mentioned in the Buckhurst Terrier (1597): 'John Alchorne holds by deed a tenement and lands called Hodlies als Milplace, 100 ac.'. The annual rent for these 100 acres was 13s. 4d.

50. Members of the Welfare family posing for a photograph during their daily work. Film was still too slow at this time to allow movement which would have been a blur on the finished picture. This is at Luxford Farm, Eridge Road, the original Manor House being concealed by additions made over the years to Crowborough's oldest building. In the Assize Rolls for Sussex of 1279 this was the residence of Bartholomew de Luggesford. The original Sussex longhouse is still contained within the brick shell covering this oldest section of the house.

51. Charity House oast house in 1926. The farm was owned by the Fermor Charity and rents from leasing the farm were used to bolster funds to run the Sir Henry Fermor School. Farm stock of £6,947 was mentioned in the proceedings of the Charity Commissioners in 1887 as being used to support the school.

52. Old farm on Chapel Green in 1870, with the Chapel Green Stores in the middle-distance and the *White Hart* Inn in the background.

53. Cooks Corner Farm. Carter John Brown leads his horse pulling a load of faggots which were used for fuel, especially firing ovens. The oasthouse in the background is mentioned by Richard Jefferies in *Field and Hedgerow*. Unmade roads were common in Crowborough in the early days.

54. Hoadley's Farm, *c.* 1880. The farmer shoulders his gun, and his wife appears to be dressed for her working day.

55. An Ashdown Forest farm, Red House, on Mardens Hill. Such farms were small but very important in forest life as their animals grazed the heath, and the farmers had foresters' rights and could collect litter and fire wood, all of which kept the forest tidy.

Transport

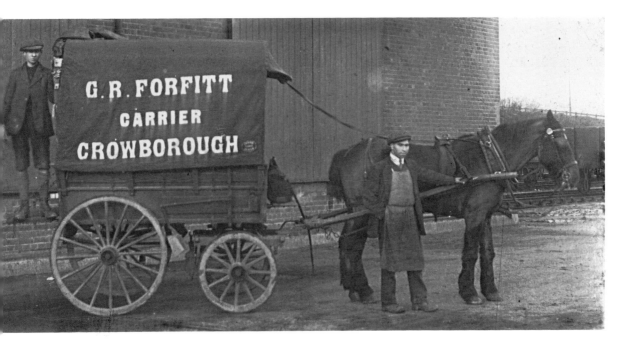

56. G. R. Forfitt, the local firm of carriers. This photograph was taken in 1922 at Jarvis Brook Station goods yard and shows Mr. Bill Chewter as driver.

57. For longer journeys Forfitt used this motor van, pictured here at Hyde Park on one of its London runs. It will be seen that it has solid rubber tyres, while the London taxi has pneumatic tyres, which had not yet been perfected for heavy vehicles.

58. Carr and Company's delivery van in the early 1900s when it appears to have won a cup in Crowborough's annual smartest vehicle competition held at the May Fair or Crowborough Fair.

59. Mr. Weston at his Croft Road property, Sandbrook House. In the background his men are cleaning a car with water drawn from a well. Later this was to be his garage and coachworks. There is now a service station and car-wash on the site.

60. Weston's coachmen pose for the camera, *c.* 1907. The men in peaked hats are taxi drivers.

61. A Model T Ford taxi with Curly Weston in the driver's seat.

62. Arthur Pilbeam in his Model T taxi in which he drove, among others, Sir Arthur Conan Doyle, who lived in Hurtis Hill.

63. A special run of the stage in 1894 meant a halt in front of the *Red Cross* Inn, now *Crowborough Cross* Hotel. This photograph recalls that in earlier times this inn was a halt for stagecoaches travelling to Brighton, but horse-changes would only be made in bad weather.

64. Martin's Beacon Motor Garage, in Beacon Road. Most of this building still exists as Caffyn's Garage. This photograph was taken in about 1912 and shows lock-up garages within the main building.

65. Workmen laying a concrete road below Green Lane on Crowborough Hill, then Station Road. The bearded man is Mr. Bassett, a well-known local man.

Public Services

66. Crowborough and District Gas and Electric Company shop at Jarvis Brook, where, close to the railway, the local gas works had its premises.

67. Men halt for a while from laying a gas main in Croft Road while they pose for the camera.

68. The Jennings both owned and ran Crowborough's hand laundry, in an old sandstone building behind Jones's fish and poultry shop. This is now a house called 'Limoru', but it was once part of a farm on the edge of open fields.

69. Members of 'The Practical Landscape Gardening and Estate Company' rest from their labours for this photograph. They were responsible for all the service work in the Warren roads, drains and sewers.

70. Crowborough horse-drawn fire engine in front of the fire station in the High Street, probably when it was first opened. Before this, the engine was kept in one of the stables opposite the *Cross* public house.

71. Members of Crowborough fire brigade, all volunteers, pose on the engine in front of Southon's shop. This building later became part of Barclays Bank and the Constitutional Club. After the club moved to London Road, the property became the Maytree tearooms of May Pinker, and now houses a kitchen planner.

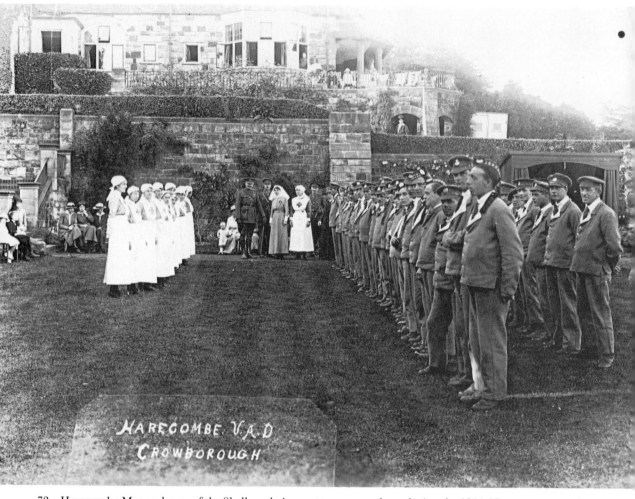

HARECOMBE. V.A.D
CROWBOROUGH

72.   Harecombe Manor, home of the Shelleys, being put to very good use during the 1914-18 war, as a convalescent home for wounded troops.

73. Just opposite Harecombe is Crowborough War Hospital. This snapshot, taken on a box camera, shows a hospital garden party in 1927.

74. Another 1927 snapshot, this time of a hospital baby show, with happy mums and healthy babies.

75. Dr. Elliot, one of a number of hard-working doctors who supported the hospital and worked selflessly for local people in many other ways.

76. Juvenile Oddfellows pose with the adult section of this popular benefit society. Before the days of state help this was the only way to ensure that poor wage earners could get monetary help, particularly in times of sickness.

Inns and Hotels

77. Club day at the old *White Hart* Inn, Chapel Green. Public houses ran clubs which paid out once a year, and enabled folk to buy expensive items such as coats or boots. On such an occasion there would be a church parade with banners. The Ancient Britons were one of the early Friendly Societies.

78. The *Boar's Head* Inn is older than the *Cross* Hotel (see plate 63) by at least 150 years. Here stage horses would have been changed before the hard pull over Crowborough Beacon, whereas the halt at the Cross served only to pick up passengers.

79. Named after an early gate through the Ashdown Forest pale, Crowborough Gate, the *Crow and Gate* Inn has a long history and was associated with smugglers. There was once a toll-gate on the site.

80. In his book, *Crowborough Hill*, Leeson Prince says of the *Blue Anchor* public house, shown here, '... the little public house called the Blue Anchor, which was the resort of various smugglers, poachers, and other lawless inhabitants of the district'.

81. *Beacon Hotel*, taken from its extensive gardens. In the background stands the Beacon post-mill, in Mill Lane, without its sweeps. The hotel was demolished to make room for new buildings, and the mill, built in 1782, was burned down in 1943.

82. *Beacon Hotel* interior, looking very plush and luxurious.

Education

83. Class of 1894, Sir Henry Fermor School, Crowborough Hill. The headmaster is Thomas Warmington, the teacher second from right is Miss E. M. Warmington, and the infants' mistress (on the far right) is Miss C. Peerless.

Crowborough
Council
School
Class 3 Girls

84.   Class Three at Whitehall National School, with their teacher Miss Clara L. Randell. This school was built in 1894 and taught 210 children. By 1897 Miss Warmington had left the Fermor school and was teaching the infants at Whitehall.

85. Empire Day and the children of St John's school salute the Union Jack. The boys and headmaster all appear to be saluting with the wrong hand so the plate must have been printed the wrong way round.

86. Steel Cross National School, built and maintained by the Goldsmiths' Company, whose crest decorates both gables. Average attendance was 100 children, and Miss Jane Fleet was mistress.

87. Pupils of Jarvis Brook School posing for their school photograph in front of the Victorian school house in 1939. The school was built in 1885 before which a farm out-building in Western Road served as a classroom. Hastingford Villa now stands on this site.

88. The original Beacon School in 1920. This school was in Church Road in the building now occupied by St Anthony's. It was a private school, but the present Beacon School is one of the largest comprehensives in Europe.

89. Parish Room, Eridge Road. Originally it was a library and working men's club, acting as a further education and leisure centre. Here it is seen as an ex-servicemen's club, probably just after 1918. A similar club stood at the top of Croham Road, where the library is today.

Religion

90. Rev. Somerville, Christ Church minister, who lived for many years at Fernbank, now the site of the Fernbank Complex and Safeways Super Store.

91. Rev. Frederick Turner, a much-loved minister of Christ Church, who with his cockatoo,'Cocky', appeared on a number of filmed perfomances on cinema newsreels. Both were well-known locally, 'Cocky' riding on the bonnet of Mr. Turner's old car, and flying up with a shriek to rest on a lamp-post if he felt like it.

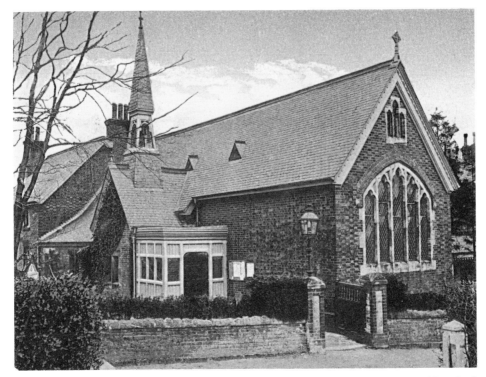

92. Christ Church on Beacon Road, built in 1879, donated to the Episcopal Free Church of England by Mrs Elizabeth de Lannoy. She also funded De Lannoy cottages, Silwood Place, and the now demolished Brincliffe. From 1879 until his death in 1900 Bishop Dicksee ministered at the church.

93. The church of St Mary Mother of Christ on Chapel Green, built in 1911. The priest's house next door was not built until 1922.

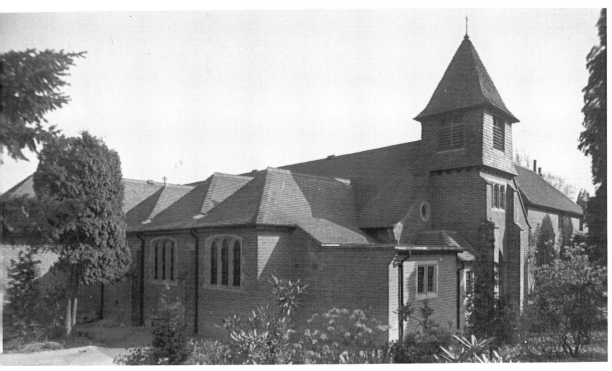

94.   The church of St John the Evangelist lends its name to the area in which it is situated, and the school opened a year after the church, in 1840. This church was built by the de la Warr family as a chapel-of-ease for St Michael's, Withyam, and was initially known as Crowborough chapel.

95.   The interior of St John's church showing the apse. Close to this church an almshouse was built by the Countess de la Warr in 1850 to commemorate the death of her eldest son, George John Frederick, Viscount Cantilupe.

96. All Saints' church and vicarage, originally the 'chapel and school' mentioned in Sir Henry Fermor's will. Building was finished in 1744, and that date can be seen on the lintel of the church door. Today only the tower is original.

97. All Saints' interior. The paraffin lamps reveal the age of this photograph, as does the organ open to public view.

98. 'Granny Brown', as she was affectionately known to the congregation and
Sunday school children of Christ Church, where she was caretaker for many years.

99. The Church Rooms in South Street, 1906. This building has now been demolished, but was used as a school hall by Whitehill, a recreation room, and for services, when it was served by the clergy of All Saints.

100. Given by the Misses Spedding of the Grange, Sweet Hawes church stood at the gates of the Grange – it was served by the clergy of All Saints.

101. The choir of All Saints' church, with Rev. Ackroyd and his curate, Mr Tonge, at the back, Mr Cannard, a coachman, on the left, and Mr Warmington, the school master who acted as bellringer, on the right.

102. St Michael's and All Angels, Jarvis Brook, as it appeared in its early days. It was built in 1906, at a cost of £2,000. Today it is surrounded by trees.

103. Ebenezer Littleton who was for many years Pastor of Forest Fold Baptist chapel in London Road. He published *A History of Forest Fold Baptist Chapel* in 1898, and was Pastor for 52 years.

104. Stanley Delves, later to be pastor of Forest Fold Baptist chapel, as he appeared in his army uniform in 1915, nine years before taking up the ministry at Crowborough. He served with the army in Russia, returning in 1919.

Parker Memorial Church
Crowborough.

Rev. A. Capes Tarbolton.
Pastor.

105. Parker Memorial Congregational church, showing its first Pastor, the Rev. A. Capel Tarbolton, 1907. This church joined with the Methodist Church (plate 107) to become the United Free Church. Crowborough's Boys Brigade is based at this church.

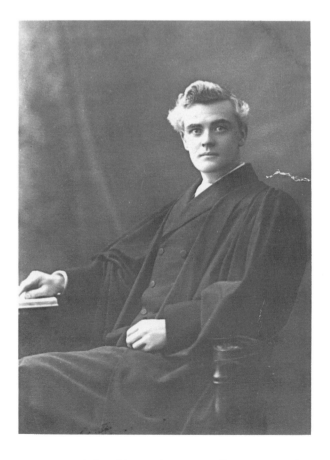

106. Rev. R. J. Campbell who did much for the Parker Memorial Church in its formative days.

107. The Methodist church in Croft Road. It still retains its Victorian appearance today, although it is now a hall, used mainly by a local play group.

108.   A very early photograph of Crowborough Salvation Army band, posing with their instruments on the south-west side of Whitehill Citadel.

Crowborough Characters

109. In later years one of the main attractions to Crowborough Cross was Jackie Lambert, born in 1898 in Queen's Road, Crowborough. This picture shows him in 1916 with a normal-sized Canadian soldier, and proves he was only 2ft. 10in. tall. The Bradley brothers, who ran businesses as tailors and saddlers in London Road, made his clothes, shoes, and other accessories.

110. Sir Arthur Conan Doyle, who moved to Crowborough in 1907. He lived on Curtis Hill in 'Windlesham', now 'Windlesham Manor', until his death in 1930. He was buried in his garden, close to the summer house in which he wrote many of his famous works.

111. Richard Jefferies, from a painting by W. Strang. His book, *Field and Hedgerow*, records much of his short time in Crowborough, where he lived at the 'Downs' on London Road.

112. Well-known Sussex cricketer, Jim Cornford, lived in the Blackness area of Crowborough, close to the Wolfe Recreation Grounds in which he practised.

113. Charlie Macey, golf professional at Crowborough Beacon Golf Club, was succeeded by his son, also Charlie, who became a well-known writer. He performed many unusual feats, recorded in the *Guinness Book of Records*, such as walking backwards to Lewes.

114. A typical Sussex countryman of his time, Tom Chewter of Crowborough Town, at the age of 93, a well-known and much-loved resident.

115. Samuel Pratt, son of Richard Pratt, at 93. They were both millers and worked Crowborough mills throughout their lives.

116. Charles Leeson Prince, pictured in 1880. Doctor and meteorologist, he stimulated the growth of Crowborough by lauding its health-giving properties in his book, *Crowborough Hill*.

117. Bert Moore, Crowborough's R.A.C. man, a familiar figure in the Cross over many years. He directed traffic in the area between 1928 and 1969.

118. A typical local businessman, Mr P. F. W. Filtness, grocer. He was the son of Mr. Filtness, of Booker & Filtness, who ran a very successful shop on the corner of the Cross where Barclays Bank now stands.

Vernacular
Architecture

119.   This old thatched cottage in Pilmer Road is fairly typical of a cottager's dwelling. One of the last of such buildings, it once stood just within Ashdown Forest, until other buildings grew around it, and heathland was cleared. Many such buildings had turf walls and heather thatch.

120. The thatched cottage in Alice Bright Lane. Legend states that Alice was murdered near here and buried at Stone Cross crossroads. Her ghost is said to haunt the road.

121. A larger than usual gardener's cottage at Sweet Hawes Grange. Its last occupant was the Grange gardener, Percy Bedwell.

122. Hoadley's Farm House, with the tenant farmer's wife and daughters posing for the camera. The house has some of the original sections still intact, though additions were made over the years, including a hand-made tiled roof replacing what once must have been thatch.

123. Crowborough Beacon golf course club house, a magnificent towered building, once in Alchornes Manor. It was demolished in 1907 to make way for a more modern building, but it still has a twin in 'Netherfield' in Crowborough Warren.

124. Mr. Stern, his coachman, and housekeeper outside Fernbank. This fine house eventually became the site for the present Fernbank Complex, the bright new centre for Crowborough.

25. Mr. and Mrs. Jenkinson pose in the garden of their home, Ocklye, in the Warren, apparently roud of their staff, including the bearded gardener.

126.   A workman stands beside the fossil he dug out of Hurtis Hill quarry. It was a Plesiosaur, evidence that this area was once roamed by dinosaurs. Fossilised footprints of an Iguanadon were also dug out from a well when Jarvis Brook waterworks were built and Conan Doyle also discovered similar fossils.

127.   This forced landing of a Bleriot-type plane at about the turn of the century had residents of Crowborough out to see just what these machines were like at close-quarters.

Curiosities

128. & 129.   Train crash at Burnt Oak in 1916. As it was war time members of the army helped the police to guard the wreckage. The crash was caused by a fast train running into a part of the line being worked on by permanent-way men. It is amazing that there were so few injuries to passengers. The driver was seriously injured. Miss May Pinker (see caption 71) was one of the passengers from Crowborough on this train, but she was not among the injured.

Crowborough
at Leisure

130.   Crowborough Cycling Club in 1902, one of the few early clubs that were for both men and women. This photograph was taken at Pilmer House, then home of Mr. Sprott, solicitor. It is now called Willetts House.

1. One of Crowborough's attractions for visitors was the shooting, mainly organised by the Goldsmiths' Company which owned much of the area in the late 19th century. Here we see tenants, farmers, guests, and beaters on the Goldsmiths' Estate before a shoot.

132. The Eridge Hunt meet, in front of Charity House, on Chapel Green c.1903. In the misty background the building of Crowborough can just be seen, rising around the Beacon. To the right is the horsetrough put up to celebrate the coronation of Edward V11 in 1902. This now stands as a large flowertub on Clokes corner.

133. Jarvis Brook football team on the coach of Sir L. Lindsay-Hogg, Bart., being honoured as winners of the Crowborough League challenge cup, 1906.

134. Crowborough Stoolball Club in the early 1900s. Third from left in the back row is Miss Daisy Stickells. This sport, peculiar to Sussex, was considered a woman's game and it wasn't until around 1945 that a few men began to play.

135. St John's Cricket Club in 1921. On the extreme right at the back is Frank Humphry, fire chief, and solicitor, of The Laurels, Eridge Road.

136. Crowborough Athletic Football Club, 1924-5, with the cups won in that year. In spite of long arduous hours at work most men found time to relax in one of the various clubs, bands, or leisure organisations of the day.

137. This almost treeless expanse is Crowborough Beacon golf course from the west, at Camp Gates.

138. This brewers' outing has travelled from Whitehill by charabanc.

139. This merry group are on an outing from Crowborough to see the British Empire Exhibition at Wembley in 1924.

40. Crowborough Beacon Brass Band, forerunners of the later silver band and present Town Band.

141. Crowds in Crowborough Broadway, *c*.1912, waiting for the Sussex bands to process past in competition. The sign on Rush's wall shows that Crowborough Hill was then Station Road.

142. The old cinema, Croft Road, 'The Picture House' once owned by Mr. A. R. Shipman of Shipman and King Theatres fame. It will be noticed it is next door to Stickells's photography shop.

Special Occasions

143. This bonfire on Crowborough Beacon would have been the final part of the celebrations for Queen Victoria's Diamond Jubilee in 1897. What a great blaze there must have been.

144. The procession commemorating King Edward's Coronation in 1902 reaches the end of Southview, with Crowborough Cycling Club leading the way. The photograph was taken from the tower of the golf club house, and shows Whincroft School in the background.

145. The May fair being celebrated in Charity Farm fields in 1923 with maypole dancing. In the background a traction engine provides energy to propel the merry-go-round. To the left of the picture and running across the background, trees hide a road which went from Chapel Green to Steel Cross.

146.   Preparing for Crowborough Carnival, 1912. The notice on the cage, in local dialect, says 'Caution – Anemiles are dangerous'.

147.   Just a few of those who dressed up for Crowborough Carnival on 4 September 1912. They were forerunners of today's Bonfire Society, who raise so much for local charities.

148. Almost finished, this large bonfire in a meadow close to the *Blue Anchor* on the Beacon is one of the early carnival bonfires.

149. The Aged Pilgrim's charity sale of work in 1915. Members pose at the Parker Memorial Church lawn, dressed as the Pilgrim Fathers who sailed on the *Mayflower*.

150. St John's school children waving flags to celebrate the end of World War I, 1918.

151. Local Boy Scouts departing to New Zealand on a special emigration scheme with their leader, Mr. Southon. It was a year when scouts all over Britain were participating in this scheme.

152. Constitutional Club, London Road, decorated for King George V's Jubilee in 1935.